READING THE BONES

JANET PAISLEY'S *Alien Crop* was short-listed for the Saltire Prize in 1996. She won the prestigious Peggy Ramsay Memorial Award in 1996 for her play, *Refuge*, as well as a string of poetry and prose awards and prizes. She has published *Pegasus in Flight* (poetry), *Wildfire* (stories) and several other plays as well as poetry and stories for children. She lives in Falkirk.

By the same author

POETRY
Pegasus in Flight
Biting through skins
Alien Crop

FICTION
Wildfire

PLAYS
Winding String
Refuge
Deep Rising
Sooans Nicht
(co-author: Graham McKenzie)

READING THE BONES

Janet Paisley

CANONGATE

First published in Great Britain in 1999 by
Canongate Books Ltd, 14 High Street,
Edinburgh EH1 1TE

10 9 8 7 6 5 4 3 2 1

The publishers gratefully acknowledge subsidy from
the Scottish Arts Council towards the publication
of this volume

British Library Cataloguing-in-Publication Data
A catalogue record for this book is available
on request from the British Library

ISBN 0 86241 884 4

Typeset by Antony Gray
Printed and bound by
The Cromwell Press,
Trowbridge, Wiltshire

FOR MOIRA
whose friendship is constant

AND FOR MY MOTHER
whose courage and love remain

ACKNOWLEDGEMENTS

My thanks to the Literature department
of the Scottish Arts Council whose award
of a writer's bursary made the writing of
this book possible, and to Judy Moir whose
editorial guidance and regular prompting
ensured its completion.

Quotes used are from *The Highwayman* by
Alfred Noyes (*The Lanimer Books of Verse
– Senior*) on p. 25 and from *Words* by
Edward Thomas on p. 34.

Some of these poems have been published in
The Dark Horse, Edinburgh Review, Nomad,
After the Watergaw, Cutting Teeth *and as*
Castlemilk Festival Love Bites *posters.*

Contents

ONE: PLUM JAM

Plum Jam   3
Mint Imperial   4
The Word   6
Tongue & Groove   8
History Lesson   11
Whist & Syrup of Figs   12
Buckled   14
Sticks & Stones   16
Avonbridge Uprooted   18
Red Hair & Biscuit Crumbs   20

TWO: LAYING TURF

Hard Currency   23
The Crow Wood   24
Leave-Taking   25
Sleight of Hand   26
Love in the Afternoon   27
Laying Turf   28
The Gift   29
Sailing with Tangled Sheets   30
The Blood   31
Cut Diamonds   32
Breaking Deep   33
Postcards from Wales   34
Disconnected   36

THREE: NINE-DAY WONDER

Glasgow Green   39
Arbroath   40
Carnoustie   40
Centre Court   41
Gracelands   41

Pinewood   42
Glen Village   43
Banknock   43
Pollokshields   44
Sunset Strip   45
Dundee   46
At Home   48
Keyed in   48
Partick   49

FOUR: CRY SAVAGE

Welsh Rarebit   53
Fig   54
Weasel   55
The Turning   57
Cry Savage   58
Desire the Leopard   60
Fruit   62
The Box   64
Amoral   66

FIVE: READING THE BONES

Snow   71
Girl   72
Mayday   73
Reading the Bones   74
Blood Sun   76
Old Warriors   78
Bird   79
Scythe   80
The Shoe   82
Lightness   83
Mountain Thyme   84
Cockade   85
Solstice   87

ONE

PLUM JAM

fruit from stone
the blood from bone

Plum Jam

She skims froth from the pot,
a wooden spoon dip and drag
through bubbling effluent.
She taps, wood claps on china.
Bland meringue, wine marbled, drops
oozing redly on the plate.

The kitchen fruits to brimming full.
Glass jars stretch a rising note
over the percussion plopping
of boiling plums poured in.

I shift the tuning fork,
turn by turn each jar sings,
clear diamond clouds to ruby
and nostrils cram with plummy heat.
Sucking moisture, I want taste.

She spins a ripe spoon.
Careful, it's hot, she says.
My lips purse, blow.
Steam snakes a slow drift round
a room sweet sour with making.

The mouthful spoons, teeth scald,
heat sticks to the roof. Wait,
she warns too late. I eat the burning.
Thick tongues of fruit lick my throat.

Mint Imperial

The round smooth white mint
nested in his palm, rare as osprey egg
sweets were. At three, the nip

of an old man, pipe tobacco stained,
malodorous as his mothballed room,
hurts. No, it doesn't, he says

when growing years add up to speech.
The brass catch on the bathroom door
catches me. He shouts,

have you fell in? Oh, yes, and drowned
please dead. Cracked leather arms
his chair, something strange slinks

where he puts my hand, movement
choreographed. Mum out of sight
at the kitchen sink.

Or in the creak of a night stair,
fevered prayers for the footfall
turning to his own bed or,

god help me, to my sister's room.
Downstairs the clack of sewing machine
doesn't hesitate. Mum stitches

a thin livelihood. I have no words
to break her thread. Tongue never
tasted mint, spat out what he gave.

Bad girl, me. So when he's gone
for a day, I crack
open his forbidden wardrobe, grab

fistfuls of round white mothballs,
cram naphthalene by pungent mouth full,
crunch and choke

hoping they'll do the dirty work.

The Word

Blistering home from school,
bursting full of — *Mam, mam,*
did you ken a dug wis a dog?
Aye, was all she said.

Discovery didn't stop. *See*
that man steys in Morag's hoose?
He's her Daddy no her Grandad.
Aye, no pause in her stirring pots.

Ah'm runnin awa door slams
did not disturb. Nothing she said,
nor Grandad with his *your heid's*
the biggest. And mine was.

Maybe something he did?
That question never asked. The word
poised tip-of-the-tongue prepared
all childhood long: *aye.*

I'd sit in templed trees, wait
to be found. No-one came. Jump
to the depth of whinstone quarry,
hoping to break. Failed again.

Lay back, cocooned in grass,
wanting to *then-they'll-be-sorry* die.
Always, stuck like a full stop
in a vast sky, a lark sang.

Who knows why children hurt,
gather stones? Weighed down, I
dragged on home, defeated by calm.
Sorry, mum — still am. Aye.

Tongue & Groove

The dog clock-watched the door,
Swiss movement accurate, and gold
coat shimmered though she stood
stock-still to conjure him.
Her cocker spaniel curse of ears
could not prick up to catch
the grinding note of downhill bus
and yet his unseen feet had just
to touch the pavement, she was off.

He'd split the afternoon soft light,
blacker than the earl of hell,
heralded by a roar. As that snarl
of pit bus gear ground up
to take the curve of main street,
through tongue and groove back door
he'd come, cast up from underground:
a man-shaped shadow furred with dust.

Pit helmet pulled off, it hunkered on
the sideboard, its glassy one-eyed glare
dared us touch, stared unblinking in
the unfamiliar light as if in shock.
Well, it had seen a dark so thick
my uncle had to breathe it in, a dark
so restless it stirred and moved
and travelled with him, a dark
that clothed. The wash was ritual.

Stripped to black vest, bare black skin,
the water ran from clear to dark,
the bar of soap frothed black. Soap
didn't do that but for him. Nobody
told him off for mess. His eyes red
rimmed were devil fierce. He scrubbed,
dog at his feet, for hours it seemed.

The sharp white bite would fade,
red eyes erase but no scrubbing
rubbed away the blackened pores.
His hands bore mourning rings,
his nails black bands. And no amount
of good fresh country air, no gardening,
hunting, fishing time, no wind could blow,
no mist or fog or rain wash out
the velvet black from coated lung.

He'd tell me that his lamp was Davy's,
canaries made sunshine down the mine
to candle-mark the coal face dark,
gas made them sing a warning. Sweat?
He worked so near to hellfire he could
hear the flames roar, feel the heat
and said small wonder the state of the vest
he'd put white on that morning.

So young I never understood a word,
I hung on every one as this rogue
brother of my mother said the queen
slept with the pope, that land belonged

to everyone, there was no god
yet the good lord put fish in the river,
game on the land for us and deer,
of course, were easier shot at night
though speaking of it brought bad luck.

A storyteller with dog and gun
who wept the poems of Rabbie Burns.
A man's a man. What else? Even yet
sky-blue eyes dance, he chuckles, grins
though it is his lungs that labour now
and *honest poverty* does not sing.
If he could buy breath, he'd scorn ownership
still. But that vest was black when they gave
it him and the lie of it proved constant.

History Lesson

depression, he said
sailed in the twenties
where the land of opportunity
steel rolled his hopes

no nigger drinks at my well
his landlady said
my grandfather saw the dust
thirsty miles walked seeking work
drew up the water
gave the cup
came back that night
found his kist packed on the porch
the door of his lodgings shut

forty years gone
he still cursed that woman
still would set the dog on
turbanned salesmen
laugh like the devil
at the rush

Whist & Syrup of Figs

The man who kissed our mother
wasn't our father and
we would not have minded but
he'd put his hands on our behinds,
act like we were dumb,
deaf and blind, would acquiesce
— wise monkeys? Truth is
he was sick and little girls
are unimpressed by adult men
whose interest wanders
down to them. At four
and five and six, we learned
quickly that a little touch
of syrup of figs
slipped in his nightly coffee
did the trick — a moving act,
so much we might have wept
until we laughed.

He taught us many things like
how to arrive en masse
at his house — a trio
who could not be prised apart
however much he tried with
you go round the shop, get
my slippers, they're upstairs. No,
you stay here! He'd get quite red
and loud — *you don't all*
need to go. Deaf, but see,

obedient. We fetched and carried
where we were sent but
synchronised. We learned
to look innocent, in unison
— spoke not one word
in our defence when asked
what we were playing at?
Dumb, see, but polite
(we thought he'd guess).

The man who kissed our mother
wasn't bright, married to
another, spent every night
in our house — losing at whist.
He'd say *that king's already out,*
he'd shout *they've fixed the cards*
while we took thirteen tricks.
We never had. At seven
and eight and nine, we'd learned
how to play for time.
And when he died, finally,
        (heart attack)
we formed a solemn crocodile
to lay a wreath, handmade as
our last laugh, from limp remains
of lovingly gathered foxglove.

Buckled

Into the corn-stalked field,
the lapwing stutters

trailing a break, buttoned
by one barbed eye, bright

as the tightly strung fence
I climb to the rescue.

Wire quakes, feet jagged this way
and that, shake. Unbalanced

the bird drags, watches, waits.
I sway, resisting the sharp top

spiked row as the foothold third
glitters a swing too far

and the fence buckles me
in and through. Barbs bite deep

into one thigh hooked skywards,
one sliding horizontal

torn unmentionably high. Wings
rise easy as the bird flies,

healed by sudden magic.
I hang hooked and bleeding

helpless, seed the yellow corn
red until I'm found, carried

home. Grimly, mother prophesies
next time you'll know

as the doctor cuts to throw away
unceremonious flesh.

There was a lesson to be learned
that day. I missed it.

Sticks & Stones

so it was you
cut me to the quick
through the separate place a child lives
far removed

screwed me down, you did
with need — the hot tobacco days
the rough caress of tweed
your big hand folded round my child fingers
— a hold that gripped
asking and receiving trust — you had
the only hands that didn't hurt

didn't hurt?
you screwed me up with sometime love
came and went
like swallows tailing summer dreams to Africa
and every time I said it — please
Daddy please don't go away
you said be brave and left

brave I was
too shocked to scream
alone and aching to fall sorely through
a winter hollowed to the bone
wanting
waiting till you came again
again were gone

and all the long time in between
inventing you, I dreamed
as skin was whipped to bleed
while childhood was invaded
when other children threw
sticks and stones and names

I grew silent
learned not to speak
learned to believe love only gives
the short swift sear of summer passion
a long season of pain and grief

Avonbridge Uprooted

Mechanical shovels scrape
the soft felt of your mossy slopes.
Torn brown welts bleed water, ooze clay,
and the tearing in my breast lays bare
the green that was my blood, turned grey.

And I am ankle deep in you,
my hands seek stone. My fingers,
searching suddenly naked boulders,
touch bone.

Once I grazed your skies,
sucked you on my tongue,
devoured you with my gaze,
filled pores with your dew.

You did not love me, expressed
disinterest with wind stroked grasses.
Your business was eternal, but you let
me share your curves, your hollows
and your wild despair.

The child I was saw risen larks
hung on crested air, wandered streams
hauntingly mocked by curlews,
made play hunting as hound
or running with the hare.

Our dreaming life understood
all but the rude stamp of steel
under the nightmare heel
of jackbooted gain

— and now it is you
laid open, wounded, raped,
made to weep black tears
down your seamed and haggard face
while the iron jaws keep crunching
and metal teeth tear flesh.

I turn from split rock, pull feet free
from this grey brown muck of you
— sun would have burned your scars
onto my sight, seared my brain
with this bruised skeleton.

Thank god for rain and, rich
as blood from bone, you rise in me.
I leave this open grave unmourned
— you are not here, and never were.

Red Hair & Biscuit Crumbs

Sandy's big brother was
the first time I came across
a brother man not boy,
tall and thin with angled bones,
said *come in* — offered
biscuits from a packet.
This, too, was new. Crisp
crinkled paper and no smell
of baking. At six years old
I could already tell
when something did not fit.
Sandy outside — the empty kitchen,
a tasteless biscuit.

Feet on the draining board
where he stood me — his red hair.
Well rehearsed, I disappeared,
remember nothing more except
Sandy's big brother was
a final confirmation. From then
I'd be just out of touch,
beyond the reach of adult men,

keeping safe — at six, removed
beyond all ordinary love.

TWO

LAYING TURF

man woman jigsaw
pieces puzzle fit

Hard Currency

The food of love, he joked
and so unlocked old dreams;
nightmares put by in pockets
of the clothes I do not wear.

But coin saved is coin there;
cold hard edges finger this
poverty of expectation. Love
does not break as bones break,

a crack. The ache of joint
disjointed heals; a face reshaped
still stares a face. But dumb
to the touch, this penny smooth

is surface and well handled,
worn and out of circulation,
exchange rate nil. Love, the last
illusion, hides in a pocket

still not gathering dust.

The Crow Wood

Book-lined, this place holds us
captive as print in pages;
a friendship fragile as thread bindings.
We thumb through us,
feelings unread as old books
bought by the yard. I want you.
Do you know that? You haven't said.
Love shouldn't be this hard.

Leave-Taking

The road is *a ribbon of moonlight.*
You, no highwayman, yet you hold me up.
Armed with the merest touch you take
all that I have left, resistance,
and make off, leaving me stripped
to a single, urgent ache.

Sleight of Hand

One smoky bar night in the green
casino light, the croupier's mask slits
empty of curious eyes. She deals chance
disinterested, takes no risk; house

limit fixed, last hand preordained.
Make your bet. The stakes are high.
Hold, play or fold, we cannot lose,
or win. He bluffs my full house

with a pair, stares me inside out.
It's how we play the game that counts.
I dare, and draw the wildcard, suspect
this deck is stacked with jokers.

He courts the jester. I catch his eye
and know he reads me like a book.
One look — he laughs, keeps his cards close
and yet, and yet . . . that rogue of chance

dances grinning in my hand, wickedness
tempts me to the blindest leap
of luck and faith and trust, to risk
it all. The chips are down. I'm in.

He calls. And once in an accidental life
we do what's right, play the cards
the way they fall, reveal our real need
to each other, show ourselves.

Love, in a foolish world, is the lord
of misrule. Both of us play the fool.

Love in the Afternoon

The sun back-lights trees,
spills onto streets, you
walk unaware of the halo
brightening your hair —
or why I smile as we play
our custom-made scenario
transparent to a fault.

Infidelity's an afternoon
strange town and restaurant
français, mais oui; an audience
self-absorbed as we — oh, yes.
The waiter knows but, bored,
he's seen too much amour, vive
la crockery — we should laugh
but don't. You ask me why
we're here and not alone.

I take you home, knowing you
hold all the barbs: your mouth,
your tongue, your hands, the thrust
of you into my centre and my soul.

No blood here, but death in heat,
that furnace-red, white-hot uproar.

And love is yet another country,
sun-lit — el dorado, matador.

Laying Turf

They came to lay turf
and stayed to smoke and talk
while the stacks curled in the heat.
Yes, there was heat
— an extraordinary Scottish day.
After tea, they worked
— two extraordinary men;
one small and brown.
Sharp as a blade, he didn't sweat.
One round and creased,
slippery in the sunlight,
who bent and laid, packed,
bent and laid, packed
— all in one unceasing move.

Next day we saw what they had made,
an ordinary miracle
— dew, fresh grass green under bare feet,
a promised morning.

The Gift

You cradle carapace
and frown, forgetting shell,
designed to crack,

will split to let
the living out. Growth erupts
through fractured husk

and the shell
was never meant to last,
however well you wore it.

Confronting birth,
I give you gifts
of time and touch,

deafened by the noise
of breaking. What is born
will not fit where it came from.

You offer me a cracked cup
which won't hold water
but it does.

Sailing with Tangled Sheets

My life is the ship in which you berth yourself,
tacking into the wind of a wilder way to be.
No harbours now, this renegade dare not dock
where madmen rattle shot across her bows.
You see the scars. Death hawks at my shoulder,
fear is a close friend. I have nothing to offer,
man, nothing but the deep rising to meet you
and my hands that will hold you from drowning.

Neither waves nor stars nor storms my making,
only the navigation of these hands on your skin,
the hunger of this mouth for the salt of you,
the ache of my womb that draws you in. Oh, man,
why do you weep when I take, and release you,
when I slow your rush for the tide? Inside,
tenderness tears me, guiding such raw need,
the swell breaking hard enough to splinter hull.

This is my element, surety of touch,
is all I have, this boat, this certain bed
sailing with tangled sheets. You give me sleep,
anchored in the blue stillness of peace, torn
from the rage of night. This in my bones,
a moment of nakedness, of knowing home.
Don't load me with futures. Just the rocking
creak of timber and this journey, all there is.

The Blood

A slow waking beats
in the vein, sucks lemon
tasted air into lungs
as the heat rises, dust
pales on black skin.

Hot, we sweat beads
of blood colours, dream
across continents,
cut wide fiery acres
from an African sky.

Here is the furnace
of our birth. Here feather,
tooth, claw, the tribal
stamp shaking earth.
A song with no words,

we are the sound
of life. The dance, fire
returning to fire, flesh
seeded from stars, suns
trapped in the bone.

Cut Diamonds

African drums thrum through my car,
beat in my blood. My headlamps cut
into the night, white-line the road,
throw back a brighter cat's eye glow;
a track of light. Guided by pin tacks,
I drive the diamond-studded dark,
race time against the black backdrop
of hill and blacker shadows. Black voices
lift my soul, and out of time and place
you fire through me, brighter far
than any light in darkness, burning deep
across the continent of my heart.

But I am driving north, away from you
and following a trail of stars.

Breaking Deep

a whole world
and you leap to straddle
its girth

move outwards   away
girdle the width
of sea

flying

the sky shot through
with rose risings

and blood-let
settings drawing light

down the drowning
red sun.

I sink in   move
under dark soil,
skin

breaking
to the burning depth

an ordinary angel   fallen
to earth

Postcards from Wales

Make me content
With some sweetness
From Wales
Whose nightingales
Have no wings.
(WORDS: Edward Thomas)

The night draws darkness down
to rest on the sea rim. Out there
where air and water reach, a boat
cuts out its own black shadow,
a silhouette lit up against the grey.

And I am here — and you are far away.

No beach surrounds me, just
a flagstoned walk, a cold and rigid
human plan of tiled desert, and a bench,
no lights, a darkened seat, unmoved,
and all around my feet a concrete bay.

And I am here — and you are far away.

No sound, the sea moves as if it were afraid.
No wind, the dusk air holds it down.
No thought, for in this fragile world
one hammer strikes the glass . . . no
wings. This is your land and yet

even as the sky that raised you
bleeds into the sea, even as
the colour drains the day . . .

And I am here — and you are far away

   . . . even as we touch —
even as we take and give too much,
even as the blood empties from my veins,
even as the imprint of your fingers
stains my skin — even as there is
no deeper in than we have been,
I cannot come to you.

And I am here — and you are far away.

Disconnected

Barefoot in the grass, damp
nets my veins to root, the mesh
that knits our surface life
connects. Above a big moon gasps
at shadows — the thread of cloud —
recovering from eclipse. My head
bursts, poems bud, flower, break
free. You do not know this me —
mad with words, crazed by silence.

THREE

NINE-DAY WONDER

a poem aches
with its own echo

Glasgow Green

Sun — hot enough to cook
kippers on stone. Heatwise,
we pass newly exposed bodies
to walk on grass. My son says
see all these men eyeing you up
next one does that I'm going to
do this — takes hold of my arm
she's-with-me possessively — *and*
ha ha ha in their face, typically
Mark. Topical, the green has gone
walkie talkie hype, mean machines
stalk the big black and beautiful
streetball crew who joke American
and work chewing gum as young
folk dream of slam-dunking and I,
of course, am not thinking of you.

Arbroath

FRIDAY

This is the silence:
the sea wrapping rock
in soft tissue — gulls peep
and wheel — soundlessly
easy in my ear. Cloud comes
down with night; out there
beacons flash such little lights
to bring the boats home.
Two days now and I haven't
thought of you at all.

Carnoustie

SATURDAY

Thirty yachts on the beach
prepare to set off — and yachtsmen,
thirty times two — bar the odd
girl or so (very odd it seems)
— sixty sun-bronzed muscle taut
sailor types, eyes on the distance
to run, circling the bay — and not
one of any interest . . . Day three
and you don't pre-occupy me.

Centre Court

Streetball finally to cheer on
a nephew's team, the melt down
drying out in the driest of heat
— a glass backboard reflects
this contest in a world become
ninety per cent male and eighty
degrees — how hot can sun be, red
hot it seems as everywhere bare
skin . . . Is it hotter than this in . . .

Gracelands
MIDNIGHT

Sunday into Monday and somewhere
between Dundee and Kincardine,
we debate light — sunrise or sunset:
too little space between to clear
the horizon with noticeable dark.
The heat has drawn moisture — sun
abandoned it lies milky in fields
— a drift destined to become fog.
Today a murderer escaped Tayside
and I left three caravanning sons to fate
for three days. David says *don't you
think it's creepy* as the vapour snakes
across the road, blinding us. You
are the last thing in my thoughts.

Pinewood

DREAM-SLEEP

You and I sit holding hands,
watching film — so predictable,
the couple tie themselves in knots
and we anticipate — *watch, this is where*
you laugh, showing off an uncanny
ability to unravel plot. And I say
here, she's going to — and she does,
infuriating us with further twists
of B-movie see-through-me action
though it's patently obvious they'll
get together in the end. We expect
and are not disappointed, when
the credits roll, to discover it was
our love-life story the film told.

Glen Village

MONDAY

Morning and the telephone rings,
your voice in my ear — your mouth
speaking my name. I am insane
with love for you, wanting to keep
the sound of you near and sit holding
the silence in my lap for hours
after you've gone — saying your name,
saying your name, replaying the tape
in my head, everything you said —
a slip of the tongue when I said I miss
you. Day five, the wonder is I was
at all able to talk. Oh, my love.

Banknock

MONDAY MIDNIGHT

This roving taxi driver
strikes the midnight oil
to collect son and girlfriend,
talking again and there,
standing under a street lamp,
an ex-lover needing a lift.
Small world, he says.
Not small enough, I think.

Pollokshields

My women are reduced to seven
while the days increase to six.
Mary trips us back to childhood,
to legs that won't reach the ground
from a swing, and muscle power
too slight to move a merry-go-round.
Inside, I'd settle for the earth
moving. At sixes and sevens, I need
food, daily bread, the taste of you.
Queen-like, Elsie May feeds us cake
and keeps her head despite the heat.
Outside, sun-burning Glasgow bakes.

Sunset Strip

TUESDAY STILL

God save us all but a certain bard,
one of only three early birds, is
stripped half naked showing off
his supertancharged torso and he
stares unflinchingly as I enter,
sit, take out my file, diary, make
some notes, greet the others and do
not look in his direction, quite
deliberate in my intention to ignore
his posturing. I'm supposed to be
impressed that in this dull room he's
spreadeagled and undressed, desperate
to catch my eye. I try to tell myself
he's a little boy wanting patted on
the head but instead his pose grates
my nerves and I know I hate this gold
edged chauvinistic bastard of a man.
So it's get tough time again (six days
without you) I've had all I can take.

Dundee

I've cracked, am speaking to
a concrete block on a stalk
and it talks back — whacky. No-one
turns a hair but three big mac meals,
go large, and the odd-one-out, appear.

Me and the lads drive our picnic
on to Camperdown — out for a lark,
they're looking for birds but no-one's
about except some french-fry fancying
Matthew-fed seagulls.

They'd pitch and putt instead but
it's shut — so, even though *we're too
old for this*, they play tig — guess
who's it? No, not me (cracked maybe
but not daft) — the wee one who can't
catch cold let alone an older (much)
brother whose legs are so much longer.

We decide on funny walk handicaps.
And me, and the stragglers in the park
and Matthew, who's supposed to be
chasing, are all doubled up, poorless,
laughing at the contorted, ridiculous
scurrying of Laurence and Mark until,
still discomposed but running fast,
the big break Matthew, intent on making

his come-back doesn't realise his shorts
are sliding down until the waistline's
at his knees — the game collapses.

Overfull of nonsense, we call it a day
(the seventh) and head for home. Guess
I'm getting used now to being alone.

At Home
THURSDAY

But on the eighth day I'm stuck
for words — the Beatles said it
wasn't enough and this is the care
you need — me here, you out there
and a whole lost world between.

Keyed in
FRIDAY

Your flat is not familiar.
It groans at the rate
of its own history, and waits.
Life gathers on the doormat
— untouched, unopened, untold.
The hands of the clock hold
absence — stuck since the last
wind-up. Trapped voices peep
like caged birds you keep
on the answer-phone. The fridge
drones a liturgy of food
uncooked and nothing good
is going on between the sheets.

Partick

rakish you are,
your revolutionary beard
bristles against my breasts.
Pillaging was never your forte
but somehow it's easy to believe
the piratical mock attack
in the dark would have any maiden
flat on her back. No doubt
protesting that she'd hate
to be deflowered in the dirt
which is why she'd lift her skirts
to facilitate the rough wooing
of this laughing reprobate.

FOUR

CRY SAVAGE

your own voice coming back
your own voice

Welsh Rarebit

He was finely chiselled.
A hunk, she said,
we shared.

Having carved him out,
buttered him up,
we ate.

Dull, we finally agreed,
not quite tart enough
for good taste.

Fig

You pick
the plumpest fruit from the dish.
A quick thumbpress
and the skin splits.
Your teeth shine,
lips blunt the razor's edge.
Tongue tucked between rim and flesh,
you suck.

I can tell from the burst
it is the best the bowl can offer.
Yet
you toss
the empty husk,
reach for another.

Weasel

He is the healer,
it's what he says, fixing us
with a green-eyed gaze of such
intense interest. Fascination
pins us to his quirky grin

and how he moves in upon us,
uninvited but oh, he is
a bonny dancer, twisting, twirling,
not one step out of place, around
us, trembling in our tender skins.

Oh, he knows the stuff
that we are made of, it's why he's here.
Once caught in cut-glass stare,
a little drunk, I thought I heard
the curling grin's sardonic lip

but, hypnotic, he is the conjuror
giving every appearance of
the oh so seductive impression of . . .
and what do we know of love?
Easy meat, me and my sons.

When it comes, the sudden leap
quite takes our breath away.
Sharp teeth he has, and quick.
A nip, a twist, a tug,
oh, always the mover, shaking

down the bloody rain.
How slowly we are standing there,
and him a blur. The teacher,
he is now tapping out the lesson of
— that tearing hair and bleeding hearts

are simply meat and drink affairs.
So all that's left, to gurgle up a laugh
save for the smallest child who weeps,
savaged and betrayed once more.
That echo mocks his parting shrug:

it's how he is. Tooth-picking flesh,
he slinks off to another feast
companioned by his pack of sweets.
It is that constant minty breath
should give his name away.

The Turning

Did you pass that old man on the stair?
An empty wind whistled through his hair
and in his ghostly eyes the icy glare
froze hard enough to crackle in my ear.

He was here, I tell you. He was here.

And was he leaving? Oh, don't turn and stare
for he lifted from the hook just over there
that overcoat of loneliness he wears.
Is that the drag of his returning I can hear?

He is near, I tell you. He is near.

What is that pungent perfume on the air?
The sour ageing in your lack of care
that beggars wanton love to raw despair
and cracks the door to draw in haunting fear.

He is here, you tell me. He is here.

Cry Savage

There were no drums that day,
no fifes, no marching feet
slow thrumming on the tarmac,
no sixty-second silence
nor any other mark. Savage

little brown birds opened throats,
gargled up a rising. Dawn
was the only thing that broke.

Brutal, the grass grew on,
greening every verge. Weeds
waved, flowering as usual
in the wrong place. I saw
people walk, cars drive the road
to work that would not wait.

Cruelly, the clouds climbed
to alleviate blue sky and peaked
too soon to drown the mockery
of a richly coloured day.

No storm, no rain, not,
at the very least,
a peal of thunder or a flash
of whiplash light to crack
a too complacent morning.

What use a god who will not speak,
what use a witch, what use
the magic arts if such a breaking
goes unnoticed, unremarked.

What use a heart, a poet's soul,
the skin that I am sitting in,
the blackest of the bleakest dark,
if all this normal, normal thing
is still intact? No scream,

no shriek, no keening wail.
Failsafe from sound, no
tuning up, no toning down, no
discordant orchestra, no band,
no brass, no blues, no all that
jazz, no pop, no hip-hop, rave,
punk, funk or folk. No joke,

it was quiet as the grave

save for ordinary birdsong
and no drum.

Desire the Leopard

This leopard who cannot change
his spots lies in my bed, sleeps
slow breathing his deep breath

rigid cold-back snore to the black
night. Next door, the roar echoes
in a silver spoon bell-spinning,
single-ringing in an empty cup.

Curtains drift, the wind uplifts
shadowed skirts of new moon riding
in a hiding sky. Nowhere, the stars

shine on. Lashed up, lid on tighter
lid, not one light eye cracks open,
the unsnuffed candle flame almost
is flickering gone and nearly dawn

has not come damply creeping
yet. The orange silk of slick skin
shifts, dark circles skirl and craik,

the fiery slitted eyes are shut
and shuttered but his grin gapes
gripping ear to ear his carved face
splits. Still, still he silent speaks,

this leopard lying smooth and surely
thrumming against my naked breast,
the hunt beat drumming of his deep

bedded heart. With claws widespread,
clear as a watershed, the drop arcs
faster than the fleetest foot
philanderer who gave this gift,

and flooding sheet hot, pillow hard
he sails the two-yard empty hollow,
hung by his own unyielding compass

leaping on to black and yellow torn
delight of newly eaten brightly red
death on licking lips. In this bed, I
know every inch, pore, hair, tooth, touch

and final kiss. He is cold comfort.

Fruit

This morning, the smell of oranges
while I drive over Kingston bridge,
as if the heat and dust of Jamaica is
nearer than grey Glasgow roofs.
Below, lurking the Clyde, no crated fruit.

This morning, the smell of oranges
is sharper than the cut of Arahova
carved in a Greek hillside, fresher
than our first stop walking barefoot
up the marble staircase we marvelled at.

A sunburst sparking orange in red earth
lit the olive groves to silver green.
We ate fat ripe tomatoes, feta,
little fish, Delphi breakfasted
on goat's milk yoghurt honeyed gold.

Old as Olympia, the spurt
of fluid from impressed skin, you,
an athlete, shared the fruit with Zeus
over the stone cartwheel disc
remains of his fallen temple:

you, stretching to pluck wild limes;
me, bending to pick up fallen figs;
a forest thundering a razzmatazz
of giant fir cones as we eased
our hunger for each other — when

in Greece. The taste is citrus, holy
as Mistra, high on its hill, baked
sand and orange stone, abandoned
and below, Sparta, its heroes gone
grey in a cardboard city cut-out.

A lie, we say, looking down
on the senseless lie of the land.
But the lie was your form, your taste,
your sound, the hand you held out
and, this morning, oranges in my car.

The Box

The box is solid as the full moon
ring shining round an ice-cloud
bigger than tomorrow, as empty as

the box, smooth as yesterday
remembered as how easy it was.
Not easy is how we forget.

The hole is dark in the space
between this world and the next
love that breaks a heart beat

timed to the world's breath. Easily
erased is the moon's flood ring
falling to a rising sun. But falling,

the hole is deeper than your words,
deep enough to hold the cut
of every bladed stroke you could not

resist adding to after you'd gone.
The moon's halo circles wider than
your letters' journeying. On the other

side of the world, you sit, nibble a pen,
draw ink from the dried well, manage
to conjure up my silence from shrieking

grief, make meaningless whatever is
played repeatedly with every note.
Licking and sticking, you don't stop

stamping into the ground. Stopping
you is a life's work in earth, scraped
damp in my fingernails. I take

the deadman speak you damn
us with, and put in, and tap down
and can dance upon

the box that is solid
the box that is smooth enough to hold

the hole that is dark
the hole that is deeper than

the earth that is thrown on
the earth that is shovelled in

the mound that is heaped over
the litany of unbelief recited as

I build up the stones
to hold you down.

Amoral

A single line and she is
heading for the off-ramp:
scrubland, brush or forest,

grass or hill, she makes
her own path, cuts
a swathe through weeds, scythes

jungle and picks leeches
from her flesh. Wild,
in the summer furnace, she

chills out on mountain water.
Man, not even in your dreams,
no more than salt-lick

to slick her tongue on,
freshen her blood on — do not
imagine you can tangle with

this woman, hunt and win. Sin
is the whetstone sharpening
her wits — she will not wear

the rights and wrongs of it.
If she comes early knocking
at your door, slide the bolt

home. Late — turn the key and in
the name of sanity keep
that chain securely fixed, do

not hear nor care, do not believe.
She'll mirror you and speak,
smile, kiss and touch as you do.

Trust? Give her nothing — not
even when she thirsts, not
warmth or food — she cannot be

trained for petting, kept
on a leash of lies or truth.
Don't be fooled, she looks beyond,

into and through, not at — no
future, she lives minutes full
as figs, splits each fleshy one,

sucks breadth and depth, draws
the outer edges in to empty skin
cast off, done. Profligate,

she lives everything she is
spread out — a resource, of joy,
of sorrow — endangered but

when the arrow of your living
slices through her, she'll escape.

FIVE

READING THE BONES

no-one to touch
fingers blind

Snow

today we make snow

flurries of white cold words
fall into silence

into that silence
deep enough to drown in

drifts drag us down
the slow slide

and sleep is an ice edge
on a frozen ledge

hunchback heaps of snow
crouch the roadside

grit shows
the sharp bite of flat blade

flayed white cuts
on crevices of brown decay

Girl

as the train rattles

along the corridor of night,
her feet clamber
the between-them table top,

small hands slip
into his cupped fingers,
easy in his touch.

Flesh of his
flesh, she is
made in his image,

adoring. Faces touch
and mouths form laughter,
a kiss. Disturbing

the light, his words
smile between them
Who do you love?

and as her sharp teeth
bite out the *You*
I bite on the erupting *No!*

and brake hard,
still angry enough
to take a whole train

apart with bare hands.

Mayday

Six other sons, and yet
I know precisely the last pull of pain
when you came out of me,
feet first, each pressured, released,
sucking like drawn plugs
and the wet, warm slither down
the drain of life.

It was the last time we touched.

You sailed beyond me,
bearing only your name.
From your glass shell, a small fist salute,
the final white box your one flag.
All you left, breast full, blood heat, the bluish milk,
fell in the void of your leaving
and destitute, my arms raged.

Such a little life,
twenty-six hours long.
Such a sore tide,
the same in years, still rising.
Time can't heal the hollow that never held you,
your absence is as a fresh wound, widening,
the salt in it your name not said.

Reading the Bones

This time it is not the child
but the man — racked and saddled
by hot sun. Over broken stone,

alone, he walks. Still upright
though burdened with the weight
that brings down worlds. Each step
is iron hard, small insects

dart in sharper shadows, cracks
open in the earth, and grief
is somewhere else — where water is.

The child he walks with is dead
yet he will not set it down.
Beyond the touch of hands, he
is merciless. Does not look back

to where he stopped last, wet
the child's mouth — a smear of mist,
the almost kiss. Does not look

forward though he goes, a slow
sure stepping toward the grave.
Proud head, straight back, the painful
ribs, stripped sticks of arms, and legs

that walk and walk and walk
and are brought down more surely
by the bones I cannot read;

bones he carries on his back.
Is it son or daughter, love
or hope, or is he saddled to
the failure of his fatherhood

— the mouth he could not feed,
the need he could not fill, a life
he could not keep — so deep a grief

it cannot be set down. On
and on into the hungry heat,
sweating flies, and every step
an agony of bone and breath.

And I am trying, blindly
to read those bones — of Man,
walking his dead child home.

Blood Sun

Already I am in summer,
two-thirds through the promised to you year.
Each hot day limps into a violet dusk.
A dull red disc, incongruous on blue,
slips into a purple pocket,
kept for another day.
We have spent our coin separately.

My way is work,
the kind that paces
evenly from place to place.
I have become a paper tiger
prowling peopled cages,
growling at the setting sun.
I wear these bars with bad grace,
bare my teeth at night's descent,
touch no-one.

And you?
Won't pluck the paper
from the fire, dare the flame.
Your winter has not moved to spring
though time spins on through summer.
The earth clock ticks. I hear
you left home, sit
in spit and sawdust bars,
drown your dreams, drink in oblivion.

Autumn, and today they buried you.

My way is work,
the kind that paces
evenly from place to place.
I have become a paper tiger
prowling peopled cages,
growling at the setting sun.
I wear these bars with bad grace,
bare my teeth at night's descent,
love no-one.

Old Warriors

Who knows what the horse hoped for?
Made for flight, but bound to rattle
life clicked out over slatted track,
shoulders burned up cart weights

of blasted coal, lungs blackened
with every deep dust breath. A breed
foreign as boys fired in the chimney,
workhouses for the pregnant young.

Yet today, two ponies come up
from a mine. Back scarred, they brace
for the flood, flinch into painful light.
Knowing nothing of mist or morning,

brittle hooves cut soil, shy from grass.
Old warriors, they stamp and snort
at the fearsome rush of acreage,
fret the lost slap of link and chain.

Adrift, day is a shifting torment
and familiar though night is,
its pit-propped roof is split, wearing thin.
The owner will sell, a thousand each,

else they're meat. No labour left
in dead beat hung bones, he counts now
on compassion as the pit ponies
worked out, reach the end of their line.

Bird

Once she'd put out
daily bread, but only crust.
Her riches more recent,
birdseed, nuts.

Now in the sterile ward,
she starves. I hold her close,
flesh like feathers,
bones like a bird.

Scythe

What we need here is
the brutality of death.
The sudden clench, the iron bite,
oh all the hunger of the chase
brought finally to fruit in one
sweet swift moment of . . .

and not the nurse.
No, not the quiet shoe, and could you
manage a little soup (the answer's no),
a cup of (no) tea (no), a sip. No,
she is not the diamorphine
fade out to a shadow of . . .

no, what we need here is
the steel door of a full stop,
the blood clot bludgeon, one
furious hot shaft of lance-like thrust
to burst through thinning membrane, cut
from life to death, the fell swoop

and not this slow bed. No, not
the bone indented pillow plumped,
the carefully adjusted drip
stitch by stitch stretching skin
over a hollow drum to beat
your victory roll on. Go on,

give us sudden shock, the mindless act
rip-roaring its triumphal passage
to an ending. Try carnage, take
the everyday way out, make your move.
Give us, this day, cruelty in
the swift bright fire, the blade.

The Shoe

A shadow burns against the wall.
The blind shoe, fit for nothing,
single on the hearthrug sits
and all the lies of ageing line
the pages of a book nobody reads.

Nobody reads. The dumb shoe speaks,
ticking off the clock on the wall
that says ten to. Somewhere a body
aches for its familiar bed, somewhere
in the sheet of night, nobody speaks.

On the sideboard all her plants thirst.
In the side ward, running out, the drip
to be turned off. The airbed creaks,
syringe pump whines a click to shake
her paper skin. The breath (wait) comes.

By the rug, the deaf shoe hears
no pages turn the book the clock reads
and woodsmoke hooks into the hall.
She said she'd lost herself as well.
Empty, the shoe. Clock reads five to.

Lightness

I enter the ward
and find her struck; a new lightning

pale on her brow.
Carefully juggled presents

trickle away like sand:
a smile, soundbite reassurance,

small pockets of word.
Grain that dusts off.

I take hold of her hands,
warm and so slender,

soft skin exposing
the departure of flesh.

The cancer grows hungry.
Soon now, it will thirst.

I give my mother all that is left,
simple touch,

an exchange of tenderness.
She is rising beyond reach

of the iron grip.
It keeps down but cannot keep.

The body fades to lightness
and however much misused the word

there is only one love.
It is at least as strong as death.

Mountain Thyme

We build a raft of heather roots
and go with you to that shore.
Wreathed in poem and song, we
thread wild thyme through your hair.

The hills, always your home,
hold steady, and proudly the pipes
announce your coming in the air.

Mouths full of ash, words done,
all that can be held now is the cord
to slip you free, and gone. We bear
the weight as you would wish us to

and pay you back into the tidal earth,
into the promise of your birth,
as you go from us. As you go.

Cockade

She gave me roses,
the white rebellion
of a fragrant history,
cut from the root.
Her own mother's, she said.

In her blood-line,
women were the word;
keepers of a tongue,
guarding womb and death.
All she could trust, finally.

And we, her daughters,
one bush. A multitude
grown in the poorest dirt,
returning the bloom.

All we could trust
silenced as she died.
Her last demand:
Ah waant an explanation
could not be met
by any god made man.

She raised the sword,
she broke the stone,
she baked the brick,
she picked the fruit,
she formed the sound,

she sang the song,
she wrote the book.

She gave me roses.
In the white rush of every June
the petals of her breath
brush my cheek.

Solstice

The pages of tomorrow wait
for word of celebration,
a stroke that calls the clock to turn
this December, drifting down,
cracks the door on blossoming.

The sting cold rivers throat and lungs,
startled in the virgin light
of a bright earth blindly wrapped
in snow and ice, the longest night
peels off for the palest sun.

The year unhinges
and all possibility is there
holding its white morning breath
outside an opening door.